Classic
AIRCRAFT

First published in 2009. A catalogue record for this book is available from the British Library

ISBN 978-1-844257-07-2

Published by Haynes Publishing, Sparkford, Yeovil, Somerset BA22 7JJ, UK
Tel: 01963 442030 Fax: 01963 440001 Int. tel: +44 1963 442030 Int. fax: +44 1963 440001
E-mail: sales@haynes.co.uk Website: www.haynes.co.uk

Haynes North America Inc., 861 Lawrence Drive, Newbury Park, California 91320, USA

All images © Mirrorpix

Creative Director: Kevin Gardner

Packaged for Haynes by Green Umbrella Publishing

Printed and bound in Britain by J. H. Haynes & Co. Ltd.

Classic AIRCRAFT

John & Richard Havers

INTRODUCTION

"Man must rise above the Earth – to the top of the atmosphere and beyond – for only thus will he fully understand the world in which he lives." – **Socrates.**

Aircraft have revolutionised the way we live. Billions of passengers take to the air every year and around the world airlines operate almost 80,000 flights daily. Before the revolution, flying was often a personal struggle in which a lone pilot and his single-engine aircraft tangled with the elements, the limits of his own endurance and the uncertainties of technology. Many of the endeavours of the early aviation pioneers ended in heroic failure. Quite a few of the aircraft pictured in these pages met the same fate.

To begin with man took to the skies in balloons, and for many years the goal of flying a heavier-than-air-machine eluded early aviators. It all changed in 1903 when the Wright brothers became the first men to fly a heavier-than-air-machine. Soon men were setting records and trying to outdo their rivals – many died in the attempt. Flying across the sea was the dream of early aviators, and while the English Channel may not have been much of an ocean Louis Bleriot's 37 minute flight between England and France amazed the world. Ten years later, in 1919, the first successful non-stop flight across the Atlantic took place when two British aviators flew the 1,890 miles from St Johns, Newfoundland, to Clifden, in Ireland, in a twin-engine biplane; it took them 16 hours and 12 minutes. It would be almost 8 years before there was another successful non-stop flight across the Atlantic: American aviator Charles Augustus Lindbergh Jr flew solo from New York to Paris in 33 hours and 30 minutes in a single-engine monoplane and became a legend.

"Aeronautics was neither an industry nor a science. It was a miracle." – **Igor Sikorsky.**

Between the two world wars the business of aviation began to develop as airlines offered travel to the wealthy few. But the limitations of technology made it a questionable mode of transport; most people stuck to ships. Popular flying in light aircraft became widespread. Air racing became all the rage and many people took their first flights in converted First World War aircraft that operated the 'Flying Circuses' around Britain. The Second World War put most civilian flying on hold, but it did have the benefit of fast-tracking the development of aircraft, enabling aviation to take a giant leap forward. Bombers produced during the war became the basis for civilian aircraft in the post-1945 world, where all things once again seemed possible. At first the opportunities for mass travel were unclear but competition between aircraft manufacturers soon began as Britain and America, in particular, raced to build the right type of aircraft for every airlines needs – and there were many. Initially Britain favoured flying boats, but quickly the opportunities for jet aircraft were identified; for a while we led the world with the De Havilland Comet. However, the Brabazon became the first in a long line of British civil airliners that helped redefine the term 'white elephant' – a political crisis was in the offing. With a shortage of British-built aircraft, the only choice for the British Overseas Airways Corporation (BOAC) was to buy American-made aircraft. Not only was this a blow to national pride but it helped the Americans gain a stranglehold on world airlines for many years – with of course the exception of the Russians.

These pages are a fascinating timeline of aviation, spanning a little over a hundred years. From flying barely faster than people could run we've been supersonic, we've taken off vertically, in confined spaces and more conventionally with hundreds of our fellow beings. We've flown solo in tiny planes, travelled over vast distances and set records that still attract people wanting to beat them. Flying manages to maintain a romantic grip on our imagination even if the reality of air travel in a tightly packed low-cost airline seat is anything but. Before we head off into the wild blue yonder don't we all secretly imagine flying first class in a flying boat while a steward in an immaculate white cotton jacket offers to mix us a cocktail?

"You want to know if this old airplane is safe to fly? Just how in the world do you think it got to be this old?" – **A very old captain.**

The caption date for each picture is generally when the aircraft was built. However, in a few, obvious, instances it refers to a specific event that is recorded by the photograph.

The Hon. Charles Rolls with his Balloon *Enchantress* at Chelmsford, following a race from Ranelagh Pleasure Gardens, Chelsea. Balloon flight began in 1783 with the brothers Montgolfier; it became a popular activity in Edwardian times, shortly before the advent of powered flight.

Louis Bleriot was the first man to fly across the English Channel in a powered aircraft. Here he is photographed, along with his wife and his Bleriot XI, on cliffs near Dover Castle after making the crossing on 25 July 1909. He left Baraques near Calais at 4.41am, completing the 26½ mile flight in 36½ minutes to win the prize of £1,000 for being the first to accomplish one of man's great aviation challenges.

On 22 February 1909 Wilbur Wright demonstrated his Model "A" *Old Personals* to King Alfonso of Spain at Pau in France. Orville Wright's *Flyer 1* completed the first successful controlled, powered and sustained flight over a distance of 120ft in 12 seconds from Kill Devil Hills, Kitty Hawk, North Carolina on 17 December 1903. The only surviving Model A can be seen in the Deutsches Museum, Munich, Germany.

On 16 October 1908 American-born Samuel Franklin Cody completed the first officially recognised flight in Great Britain, at Farnborough in Hampshire. This photo was taken a year later to the day, when he flew at Doncaster racecourse at an air display that had attracted 100,000. Though he crashed there, he was unharmed. But his luck ran out on 7 August 1913 when he was killed in an accident on Laffan's Plain, Farnborough. The smaller picture shows Cody with his wife on 16 August 1909 when she became the first woman to have a flight in a 'heavier-than-air-machine' at Laffan's Plain.

The Hon. Charles Rolls, holder of Royal Aero Club Certificate No.2, is seen here flying his French-built Wright biplane during Bournemouth Aviation Week in July 1910. He was killed on 12 July while taking part in a competition for the slowest lap; part of the aircraft's tail-plane collapsed and he crashed from just 20ft. On 2 June 1910 Rolls had completed the first return flight across the English Channel, dropping a letter addressed to the Aero Club de France before he flew back to England.

1 9 1 0

Carl Fisher was the owner of the first American automobile dealership in Indianapolis; he is seen here piloting a balloon over the city's downtown area with a Stoddard-Dayton motorcar suspended beneath it. Unbeknown to people on the ground, to save weight the car was without an engine, but, on landing, Fisher drove a similar car back into town claiming that it was the one seen in the air. He then ran an advertising campaign claiming, "The Stoddard-Dayton was the first automobile to fly over Indianapolis. It should be your first automobile too."

A V Roe, one of the early pioneers of British aviation, test-flying the second Roe 1 triplane at Wembley Park in January 1910. Its 20hp JAP engine was sufficient to allow circuits of the airfield with few mishaps. The first triplane is now in the Science Museum, London, while a replica of his first design, the Roe 1 biplane, can be seen at the Brooklands Museum in Surrey. A V Roe here stands next to his triplane.

1910

Distinguished British aviation pioneer Claude Graham-White, accompanied by a lady passenger in his Henri Farman biplane, probably at Hendon, Middlesex. In April 1910 Graham-White completed the first night-flight in Britain while attempting to overtake a rival during the London to Manchester air race.

Colonel J T C Moore-Brabazon (later Lord Brabazon of Tara) preparing to fly a Voisen-Farman I bis. On 2 May 1909 at Leysdown, Isle of Sheppey, he became the first resident Englishman to complete a solo aeroplane flight in England; he flew 450ft in a Voisin biplane fitted with an eight-cylinder ENV engine. He was also the first Englishman to hold a pilot's licence: he was issued No.1 licence by the Royal Aero Club on 8 March 1910. He gave up practical flying in 1910 but continued to be closely involved with aviation until his death, aged 80, in 1964.

Victor Console, a *Daily Mirror* staff photographer, flew across the Alps in a balloon in August 1912, accompanied by a Captain Spelterini. They started from Interlaken, flying to Unter-Ammergaii, a small village in Upper Bavaria, where police detained them. After being kept under close observation for an hour and a half, the two aeronauts were released; it was presumed at the time that they were detained because of the "spy" mania then prevalent in Germany. The picture shows the start of the flight, with the Jungfrau Mountain in the background.

1912

This Blackburn Kangaroo, a former First World War bomber, was purchased by explorer Captain, later Sir, Hubert Wilkins to compete in a race sponsored by the Australian Government; a prize of £10,000 was offered for the first all-Australian crew to fly from England to Australia. Piloted by Lieutenants Val Rendle and D R Williams, with Wilkins as navigator and Lieutenant Potts the engineer, the aircraft left Hounslow in West London on 21 November 1919. It suffered a serious oil leak on 8 December and returned to Suda Bay, Crete, where the flight was abandoned.

Despite appearances, this was the end of an amazingly successful flight. This Vickers Vimy bomber piloted by Captain John Alcock with his navigator Lieutenant Arthur Whitten Brown had flown across the Atlantic from St John's, Newfoundland, in 16 hours, 27 minutes. Alcock and Whitten Brown had made the first non-stop crossing of the Atlantic, crash landing on Derrygimla bog at Clifden, County Galway, Ireland on 15 June 1919: they won the £10,000 prize for their 1,890 mile flight. Although the Vimy tipped on to its nose neither man was injured. Both were knighted by King George V, but Alcock died a few months later while attempting to land in fog in France. This Vimy is exhibited in the Science Museum, London. In 2005 Steve Fossett and Mark Rebholz flew a replica across the Atlantic.

During a transport strike in the autumn of 1919 airfreight came into its own for the first time. The *Daily Mirror* were quick off the mark and used up to 12 aircraft, including this Handley Page 0/400, to deliver newspapers to Lincoln, Plymouth, Weston-Super-Mare, Liverpool, Leeds, Cardiff and Newcastle. Here copies of the *Daily Mirror* are being unloaded at Newcastle-upon-Tyne on 30 September 1919 after a three hour flight from Hounslow in Middlesex.

This Farman F-60 Goliath France, a former French First World War bomber with its box-like fuselage, was eminently suitable for conversion into a 12- or 14-seat passenger airliner. Large picture windows were added, making it one of the most successful early commercial aircraft. In late January 1919 Henri Farman took journalists on a flight to demonstrate the possibilities of sophisticated air travel. It was a Farman that flew the first regular international passenger service between Paris and Brussels on 22 March 1919; although the airline had flown a Paris-London (Kenley) service on 8 February this was not recognised since the passengers were military personnel and civil flying after the First World War was not yet

A De Havilland DH4A of Air Transport & Travel Ltd, which made the first daily international air service by a British airline when it flew from Hounslow, London, and Le Bourget, Paris, on 25 August 1919. Four of these converted First World War bombers were used by the company. The first one completed its flight in 2 hours 30 minutes, carrying a consignment of grouse, newspapers, leather and Devonshire cream along with G M Stevenson-Reece, a newspaper reporter. The company went into liquidation in December 1920 as a result of subsidised low fares charged by foreign airlines.

The R 33 Airship and its sister ship were virtual copies of a Graf Zeppelin that had been brought down by anti-aircraft fire in 1916. This huge craft with a length of 633ft and a diameter of 78ft is seen here approaching the mooring mast at Croydon during July 1921. In 1921 the Imperial Conference was held in London: this was considered an ideal opportunity to demonstrate how airships could link the countries of the British Empire. The R 33 was engaged in trials all over the country from its base at Pulham in Norfolk, and so a wooden mooring mast 140ft high was built at Croydon; it was used only twice before it was removed in September 1921, having been built on private land without permission.

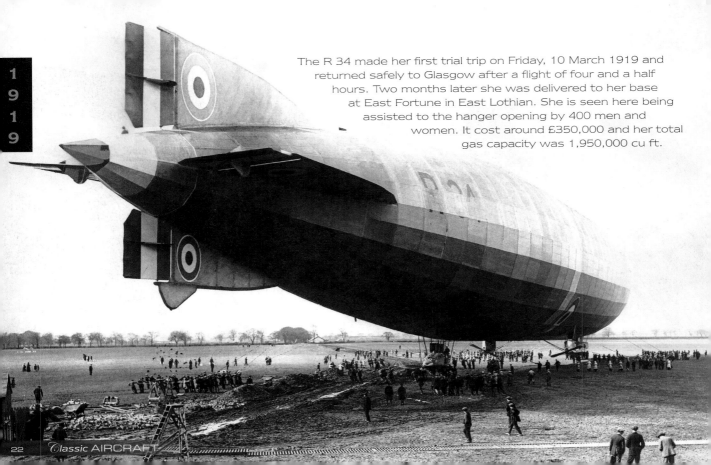

The R 34 made her first trial trip on Friday, 10 March 1919 and returned safely to Glasgow after a flight of four and a half hours. Two months later she was delivered to her base at East Fortune in East Lothian. She is seen here being assisted to the hanger opening by 400 men and women. It cost around £350,000 and her total gas capacity was 1,950,000 cu ft.

1919

This Avro 504L seaplane, a former First World War wooden trainer, was widely used, mostly with a wheeled undercarriage, by numerous companies and individuals for joy riding from 1919 to the mid-1930s. The Avro 504 was the aircraft type in which so many people experienced their first flight. This picture was taken in the Isle of Wight during August 1919 where Captain F Warren-Merriman was flying one of a large fleet operated by the Avro Transport Co.

1919

This Airco DH-4 operated a service from London's Croydon Airport to Paris. Instone & Co. were a shipping company that originally operated a private service from their base in Cardiff via London to Paris late in 1919. The London to Paris segment was turned into a public service in April 1920 under the name of Instone Air Line.

1920

This Gloster Mars Bamel piloted by Captain Jimmy James, the test pilot of Gloster aircraft, is taking off from Hendon at the start of the Aerial Derby on 16 July 1921, a month after the aircraft's first flight. The race went from Hendon to Brooklands and Epsom in Surrey and from there to West Thurrock and Epping in Essex before returning to Hendon, via Hertford. Jimmy James won the race with a speed of 163mph; the Home Secretary presented him with a trophy and prize money of £600 – worth over £50,000 in today's values.

This Aero-Lloyd Dornier Komet II was the first German commercial aircraft to visit the United Kingdom since the First World War. The all-metal aircraft with a 6000hp BMW engine and a maximum speed of 124mph, carried six passengers. It brought three Aero-Lloyd directors to visit Daimler Airways to finalise arrangements for a London–Berlin service. The Komet II had flown from Berlin via Amsterdam and Rotterdam, and due to bad weather landed in a field near Lympne in Kent, where crew and passengers spent the night before arriving at Croydon Airport.

Four Douglas World Cruisers, modified torpedo bombers named after the cities of Seattle, Chicago, Boston and New Orleans took off from Lake Washington, Seattle, on 6 April 1924 and headed west to fly around the world. *Seattle* was lost when it hit a mountain in Alaska. Pictured here is *Boston* with Lieutenant Lowell H Smith, the leader, and crew when they arrived at Croydon on 17 July; later it force-landed in the Atlantic, with the remaining two arriving back in Seattle on 28 September after their 27,534 mile flight over 28 countries.

1924

Sir Alan Cobham climbing out of
a De Havilland DH50 at Croydon
Airport on 17 March 1925. He had
returned from a trip of 17,000
miles with Sir Sefton Brancker,
the director of civil aviation, which
had taken them almost four
months. Brancker had gone to
India to report on the possibility
of establishing facilities there for
airships. Cobham was shocked to
learn that Brancker was to travel
by sea, because of government
budgetary constraints, and so
the aviator raised the finances to
enable him to be flown instead.
They left Stag Lane aerodrome
in North London on 20 November
1924, travelled through Europe
at a leisurely pace before arriving
in Karachi at the end of the year.
After India, Brancker decided
to go on to Rangoon, Burma,
from where the return journey
commenced on 28 February.

This Breguet 19A-2 open-cockpit biplane was the most celebrated French long-distance aircraft of the twenties, making many flights including two crossings of the Atlantic. The *Asahi Shimbun Corporation*, a Japanese newspaper, imported Breguet J-KIKU *Hatsukaze* (*First Wind*) and J-KIRI *Kochikaze* (*East Wind*), which were flown from Tokyo to Paris in July 1925 by Japanese pilots Abe and Kawashi; their later tour of Europe included a stop at Croydon Airport, where this photo was taken.

The Short Crusader went to Venice for the 1927 Schneider Trophy; seen here at Felixstowe, Suffolk, it crashed on 11 September in Venice while being used as a practice aircraft. The first Schneider Trophy was held in Monaco in 1913 and was introduced for aircraft that could operate from water; the principal competitors were America, France, Great Britain and Italy. In Venice the 50km race was won by a British Supermarine S5.

Captain Charles A Lindbergh's *Spirit of St Louis*, a Ryan NYP single-engine monoplane, arrives at Croydon on 30 May 1927 from Paris via Brussels. Lindbergh was met by the largest crowd ever gathered at an airport to meet an incoming flight. On 20 and 21 May 1927 he made the first solo non-stop crossing of the North Atlantic, from Long Island, New York, to Paris (Le Bourget) in 33 hours, 39 minutes. He covered a distance of 3,590 miles to win a prize of $25,000. This aircraft is exhibited in the Smithsonian Institution, National Air & Space Museum in Washington, DC.

1927

This Fokker FVIIA named *Princess Xenia* is surrounded by crowds before leaving Baldonnel Aerodrome, Dublin, on 16 September 1927 on an attempt to cross the North Atlantic from east to west. Flown by Imperial Airways Captain Robert H M MacIntosh and Commander James Fitzmaurice of the Irish Air Corps, it failed after being forced back by a gale over the Irish coast. A year later Fitzmaurice made a successful attempt in a Junkers F13 with a German crew.

Sir Alan Cobham's Short S5 Singapore 1 flying boat left the River Hamble near Southampton on 20 November 1927 for an African Survey Flight. Cohham routed via Bordeaux, Marseilles and Ajaccio to Malta, then via Entebbe and the east coast of Africa, arriving in Cape Town at the end of March 1928. His wife and two crew accompanied him, and they continued on 3 April, via the west coast of Africa, eventually arriving in Plymouth on 31 May 1928. The photo shows the Singapore in Ajaccio harbour.

This Supermarine S6 seaplane was Britain's entry in the annual Schneider Cup races. Here, R J Mitchell, the aircraft's designer, is supervising work by searchlight at Calshott in August. The S6, flown by Flying Officer H R Waghorn, went on to win the race at an average speed of 328.6mph. Much that was gained from the design and operation of these racing aeroplanes went towards the success of Mitchell's Supermarine Spitfire.

The Olympia International Aero Exhibition was first held in 1909, resuming in 1920 after the First World War and continued in this form until it eventually became the familiar SBAC Show, now held at Farnborough in Hampshire. Pictured top right is the Supermarine S5, winner of the Schneider Trophy in Venice the previous year.

On 18 June Amelia Earhart, the first woman to fly across the North Atlantic, arrived at Burry Point near Llanelli, Carmarthenshire, at 12.40pm after a 20 hour, 40 minute flight. Commander Wilmer Stultz, accompanied by engineer Lon Gordon, flew the Fokker F-VIIA-3m, named *Friendship*, with Amelia, an experienced pilot, navigating for much of the way. They left Trepassay Harbor in Newfoundland at 3.50pm on 17 June and experienced a difficult crossing with rain, dense cloud and severe turbulence. They are photographed leaving Burry Point for Southampton, their original destination.

This Fokker F-VIIA *Princess Xenia*, which had been used on the abortive transatlantic flight by Captain MacIntosh in 1927, is seen here landing at Croydon Airport on its return from a record-breaking flight from India to the UK in September 1928. Captain Barnard and Flying Officer Alliot flew the 5,000 miles in four and a half days – two and a half days faster than the record set the previous year.

Squadron Leader Bert Hinkler, photographed beside his Avro 581E Avian, made headline news when he left Croydon on 7 September 1928 to make a historic flight to Darwin, Australia. Despite having to service the aircraft himself, he still managed to average 650 miles a day and reduce the flight time between England and Australia from 28 to 15 days. He was later awarded the Air Force Cross for achieving the finest aerial exploit of the year. The Avian is preserved in the Queensland Museum, Brisbane, Australia. Three years later, while making another solo flight to Australia, Hinkler crashed in Italy and was killed.

The Graf Zeppelin D-LZ127, powered by five Maybach 550hp engines, was 776ft long and had a volume of 3,300,000 cu ft. During the 1920s Dr Hugo Eckener, the greatest of all airship pilots, raised the money to build the Graf Zeppelin which first flew on 26 April 1928. It was on 11 October 1928 that the first of over 100 transatlantic flights left Friedrichshafen, Germany, for Lakehurst, New York, carrying a crew of 40 and 20 passengers. During 1929 a round-the-world trip of 21,500 miles was completed in 20 days. The airship is photographed here over London on 4 April 1930 en route to Cardington, Bedfordshire.

1929

Fokker FVIIA G-EBTS *The Spider* was the old *Princess Xenia*. Bought by Mary, Duchess of Bedford, the craft was renamed *The Spider* after the legend that inspired Robert Bruce – to try, try and try again. With Flight Lieutenant Charles Barnard and co-pilot and navigator Robert F Little, the Duchess set off from Lympne in Kent on 2 August and arrived back in Croydon on 9 August; the last leg from Sofia took 13¼ hours. This proved that a flight to India and back could be done in eight days.

R 101

G-FAAW

G

R 101

G

The R101,
777ft long with
a total volume of 5.5
million cubic ft, was built by the
Air Ministry for the Imperial Airship Scheme. It first
flew on 14 October 1929, but subsequent test flights revealed numerous design faults. It is
photographed here before setting off on 4 October 1930 from Cardington, Bedfordshire, to
fly to Egypt and India. Early the next morning over Beauvais, near Paris, an unexplained dive
caused the airship to strike the ground. From the 54 persons aboard only six survived; the
dead included Lord Thompson, secretary of state for air, and Sir Sefton Brancker, director
of civil aviation. This was a devastating blow to the plan to introduce airships across the
British Empire, all further development was then abandoned.

The *Southern Cross*, the three-engine Fokker VII-3m made the first crossing of the Pacific Ocean from Oakland, California, to Brisbane, Australia, via Honolulu and Suva, Fiji, in a flying time of 83 hours 38 minutes in May 1928. It was flown by Australians, Captain Charles Kingsford-Smith and C T P Ulm. It's photographed here at Portmarnock Beach, Ireland, shortly before becoming the second aircraft to make a non-stop east-west crossing of the Atlantic. It left at 4.25am on 24 June 1930, landing at Harbour Grace, Newfoundland, after a somewhat difficult flight of 31½ hours. Kingsford-Smith subsequently made further record flights and received a knighthood in 1932.

The Dornier Do-X flying boat was built at Altenrhein, Switzerland, by Aktiengesellschaft fur Dornier-Flugzeuge. It was the largest, heaviest and most powerful flying boat in the world when it made its first flight on 25 July 1929. Conceived by German constructor Dr Claudius Dornier, it took seven years to design and a further two to build and was said to be the first aircraft in the world to have a wooden mock-up made before production. It carried 150 passengers plus a crew of 10. It is photographed here prior to a transatlantic flight, which left Friedrichshafen, piloted by Captain Christiansen, on 2 November 1930. It was damaged en route at both Lisbon and the Canary Islands, finally arriving in New York almost a year later on 27 August 1931; the return flight left on 19 May 1932.

An Armstrong Whitworth AW-154 Argosy, *City of Glasgow* of Imperial Airways, a three-engine that could carry 20 passengers. Photographed on Monday 4 August 1930, it brought Amy Johnson back to the UK after her record-breaking solo flight to Australia in May. She had left Croydon on 5 May and arrived in Australia on 24 May, a flight of 11,000 miles; she was the first woman to make the trip alone.

The record-breaking Vickers 142 Vivid was a two-seat, general-purpose biplane with a 590hp engine. Initially flown as a seaplane before conversion to a landplane, it is seen here with Captain Neville Stack and John R Clifton prior to departures from Heston, West London, during 1931 on the first of a series of record-breaking return flights to Berlin, Copenhagen and Warsaw. The Vivid was later destroyed during a hangar fire at Broomfield Aerodrome, Chelmsford, Essex.

A Handley Page W-8 banks over the parked aircraft at Cramlington airfield. Four of these aircraft were built for Imperial Airways and could carry 12 to 14 passengers with a range of 500 miles at around 100mph. The aircraft were gathered at Cramlington following an air race from Heston in May 1931. Between the wars air races were extremely popular, attracting large crowds wherever they were held.

The De Havilland DH82a Tiger Moth is probably the most well known two-seat trainer biplane of all time. It first flew on 26 October 1931 and can still be seen in many parts of the world today. Built in vast numbers during the Second World War in the UK, Australia, Canada and New Zealand, it is powered by a DH Gipsy Major engine. Here Evangeline Hunter-Jones takes her first flight with daughter Georgina at the controls in aid of the Women's Cancer Control Campaign on 6 May 1988.

1931

The Comper Swift, a single-seat sporting aircraft, photographed at Heston in West London for the start of the King's Cup Air Race on 26 July 1931. Flown by Squadron Leader J R Robb (later Air Marshal), it achieved sixth place at 118.3mph. The first King's Cup air race, presented by King George V to the Royal Aero Club to encourage sporting flying in Great Britain, took place on 8 September 1922 from Croydon via Birmingham, Newcastle, Glasgow (the overnight stop), Manchester, Bristol and returned to Croydon, a distance of 810 miles. The race continues annually to this day, but is flown over a course of 100 miles.

1931

G-AAZF

34

Flying Officer Snaith in Supermarine S6B on 13 August 1931 in high-speed trials for the Schneider Cup races. Britain was the only country able to provide an aircraft and so won the cup in perpetuity when the other Supermarine S6B, S1595, flown by Flight Lieutenant J N Boothman, flew around the course at Calshot, in the Solent, at a speed of 340.08mph on 12 September.

The Armstrong Whitworth AW15 Atalanta was named *Amalthea*; in the days when aircraft and especially airliners were still regarded as ships of the air they were almost all given names. Only eight were built, able to carry 17 passengers and three crew, for Imperial Airways for use on the Nairobi–Cape Town and Karachi–Singapore sections of the trunk routes to South Africa and Australia. This was the second to be built and was captured in August during an early test flight before delivery. *Amalthea* was lost in an

Eight of this supremely elegant Handley Page HP42 four-engine biplane were built. Able to seat 38 passengers, they were introduced into service by Imperial Airways in November 1931; four operated services to Paris (the Silver Wing) and other European capitals, while the remainder flew from Cairo on routes to India and South Africa. *Heracles* and other names from history and mythology were used, aptly describing these giant airliners, which remained in service until the early days of the Second World War. In this photo Arsenal footballers are seen departing on the 12.30pm flight from Croydon to Paris to play against the Paris Racing Club, on 30 October 1932.

1932

Amelia Earhart became the first women to complete a solo flight across the North Atlantic when she and her Lockheed Vega completed the journey on 21 May 1932. She left Harbour Grace, Newfoundland, on 20 May, the fifth anniversary of Charles Lindbergh's first transatlantic solo flight. Her flight nearly ended in disaster as she encountered severe storms and problems with the aircraft. She was bound for Paris, but with fuel running low she instead landed in a meadow near Londonderry, Northern Ireland. She is pictured here at Hanworth aerodrome, West London after arriving from Londonderry in a De Havilland Puss Moth chartered by Paramount News. In 1937 she disappeared in mysterious circumstances while making an attempt on a flight across the Pacific.

The De Havilland DH80A Puss Moth *The Heart's Content* with a DH Gipsy Major engine over the Atlantic with Jim Mollison at the controls. Mollison was making the first solo east-west crossing of the North Atlantic on 18-19 August 1932. Leaving from a beach at Portmarnock, just north of Dublin, he made the crossing in 31 hours 20 minutes, landing at Pennfield Ridge, New Brunswick. To give it the necessary range of 3,600 miles the aircraft was given a 160-gallon fuel tank and extra windows; Mollison sat behind the fuel tank. It was one of the greatest solo flights – the first in a light aeroplane, the fastest and longest non-stop flight. Puss Moths can still be seen flying today.

The De Havilland DH84 Dragon fitted with two 130hp DH Gipsy Major engines was conceived as a twin-engine equivalent of the Fox Moth. This six passenger aircraft was ordered by Hillman Airways to be used on their service to Paris. Some 115 were built in Britain, with a further 87 built in Australia, and were used extensively by the airlines of the 1930s. This one is photographed on a survey flight over the Shetland Islands in 1933; a few survive today.

1933

This De Havilland DH84 G-ACCV, named *Seafarer*, was specially equipped with cabin fuel tanks and strengthened undercarriage for an attempt by Jim Mollison and Amy Johnson, the husband and wife aviators, on the world's long-distance record. The couple took off from Pendine Sands in South Wales on 22 July 1933; here they are photographed over Galley Head Lighthouse, County Cork, Ireland, heading out over the Atlantic en route to New York. After a flight of 39 hours they arrived over Bridgeport, Connecticut, but owing to fatigue and darkness they landed downwind, turning the aircraft over; they

The Boeing Stearman 75 two-seat biplane began life in America during 1934 and became one of the main wartime trainers of the US Air Force. Fitted with a variety of radial engines they found use post-war as a crop-sprayer, trainer and in private use, which continues today. Shown here are Sara Mozayeni and Jullette Pendleton, wing walkers of the *Utterley Butterly* team over Gloucestershire in July 1999.

The De Havilland DH89a Dragon Rapide was first flown from Stag Lane by Hubert Broad on 17 April 1934; eventually 728 were built for civil and military use, seeing service in most parts of the world. With Gipsy Queen engines and seating for 8 to 10 people, the aircraft gave many a person their first flight. Around 40 survive, with a few still flying today. Two of the survivors are photographed here at the Wroughton air show in August 1993.

The De Havilland DH88 Comet with two DH Gipsy Six engines was conceived as a racing aircraft. In 1933 when the Victorian Centenary Air Race from England to Melbourne, Australia, was announced, the idea for the Comet was born and three were built and entered. The eventual winner of the speed prize was G-ACSS *Grosvenor House*, flown by C W A Scott and Tom Campbell Black, in 70 hours 54 minutes. Shown here is G-ACSS at the Wroughton air show in August 1993.

The De Havilland DH87b Hornet Moth side-by-side, two-seat cabin biplane with a DH Gipsy Major engine became a popular touring aeroplane. Some 165 were built and some 15 are still being flown regularly today. Photographed at the Wroughton air show in August 1993.

Airspeed AS5A Courier was an all-wooden six-seat monoplane fitted with an Armsrong Siddeley Lynx IVC engine. Designed originally by A H Tiltman for Sir Alan Cobham to make a non-stop refuelling flight to India, it was the first British-designed aircraft to be fitted with a retractable undercarriage. This one, photographed at Hanworth aerodrome in West London during 1934, belonged to London Scottish Provincial Airways, which operated routes from London to Scotland via the Midlands.

THE CIERVA AUTOGIRO COMPANY L?

G—A·C·L·T—

This Italian-registered Fokker FVIIB-3m I-AAIG, a more powerful version of the eight-passenger airliner, was fitted with three 330hp Whirlwind J-6-9 radial engines. This one belonged to the Italian company Ala Littoria and was photographed in Somaliland; it was normally based at Asmara, Eritrea. The aircraft was lost during the Second World War.

Gonzáles Gil-Pazó GP II was built in Spain by Arturo González Gil y Santibañez and José Pazó Montes. This special version was fitted with a single 130hp engine. It took part in a record attempt from Barcelona to Senegal, piloted by Ramon Torres and Carlos Coll of the Aero Club Aero Popular de Barcelona, but landed in Morocco after cross winds affected its flight. It is photographed here at Madrid airport during test flights, where it proved it could average a speed of 250km with a range of 2,000km; it was destroyed in an accident at Los Alcazares in January 1937.

This Royal Aircraft Factory SE5A was a former First World War fighter, converted in 1923 by the Savage Skywriting Co. Ltd at Hendon to be one of its fleet of skywriting aircraft. Using smoke canisters to "write in the sky", this was a popular means of advertising during the 1920s and again after the Second World War; it was banned in the 1950s. Ironically, given its pedigree, this aircraft was sold to Germany in 1929, moved on to Holland in 1934 but returned to Germany in 1936. It's shown here at Heston in West London on 13 January 1936, shortly before returning to its base at Düsseldorf.

1936

Short-Mayo Composite flying boats *Mercury* and *Maia* were built in an attempt by Imperial Airways to serve the transatlantic airmail route more efficiently. The idea was to launch the heavily loaded mail plane *Mercury* from the back of the lightly loaded *Maia* after the combination had climbed to cruising level. The *Maia* was an adapted Short S30 Empire flying boat. Flying trials began in early 1938, with the first separation on 6 February and the first long-distance flight from Foynes in Ireland on 20 July. Captain Don Bennett (who became a famous Second World War Pathfinder pilot) then flew *Mercury* on to Montreal, a distance of 2,930 miles, in 20 hours 20 minutes. He later flew south to New York where *Mercury* was reunited with *Maia*. The Second World War put paid to any further development of this interesting conception.

This Lockheed 10A Electra, a 10-passenger, two-crew American-built all-metal airliner with two 450hp Pratt & Whitney Wasp Junior R-985-SB2 radial engines, was used by British Prime Minister Neville Chamberlain to fly to a meeting with Hitler in an attempt to resolve the Czechoslovakian crisis. The British Airways aircraft left Heston on 15 September 1938 and flew to Munich.

This Bloch 220 16-seat airliner with two 985hp Gnome Rhone engines gained the unofficial *Blue Ribbon* record on the London-Paris service, which it had begun to serve on 27 March 1938. Air France operated a total of 16 of these advanced airliners; some survived the Second World War to appear again at Croydon Airport after the conflict. This Air France Bloch 220 was photographed at Croydon in 1939, with an Italian built Savoia Marchetti S73 three-engine airliner in the background.

Despite the serene scene surrounding this Spartan Arrow, a two-seat private and club aircraft built in 1933, the aircraft had been involved in a fatal drama in September 1933 when its first owner, Lady Clayton East Clayton, fell out on take-off and was killed. Six years later Mrs Gabrielle Patterson, a flying instructor and leader of the Women's National Air Reserve, was giving instruction to fellow members at the Romford Flying Club at Maylands aerodrome in Essex. She was among the eight pilots selected in 1940 to form the first unit of women in the Air Transport Auxiliary (ATA) that ferried aircraft during the Second World War.

This Miles M14a Hawk Trainer 3 was a two-seat aircraft fitted with a DH Gipsy Major engine. First flown in 1937 it saw some civil use before being built in large numbers for training military pilots during the Second World War; post-war it was extensively used by flying clubs. Pictured here is a pre-1939 example flown during the 1950s by Doug Bianchi from White Waltham along the route of the Thames.

The Cessna C-165 Airmaster was an American four-seat cabin monoplane first produced in 1935. The C-165 version appeared in 1940 and was the forerunner of a long series of very successful light single, twin and jet aircraft produced by Cessna at Wichita, Kansas. The example here was photographed at the Wroughton air show in 1993, and can still be seen flying today.

The Bristol Type 170 Freighter was designed with the unique feature of opening nose doors, which made it eminently suitable as a cargo aircraft. It was not long before Silver City Airways were attracted to the idea of starting cross-channel services for cars between England and France. Its first flight was at Filton, Bristol, on 2 December 1945, following which a total of 241 of all marks were eventually constructed. Pictured here is a Swallow Dorretti sports car being loaded into a Silver City Airways aircraft, probably at their base of Ferryfield in Kent.

This Vickers Viking 1B passenger airliner carried 24 passengers, the prototype of which first flew from Wisley, Surrey, in the hands of Chief Test Pilot Mutt Summers on 22 June 1945. It was the first post-war British airliner, derived in part from the Wellington bomber, and was ordered by British European Airways who eventually received around 40 for their UK and European services. A total of 168 were built and served airlines in Africa, South America, the Middle East and Europe. This British European Airways G-AIVD *Venteren* was photographed flying over the Alps in January 1950.

The Avro 685 York C1 transport was originally designed for the RAF using the wings, engines and twin-fin tail arrangement of the Lancaster bomber; it flew for the first time on 5 July 1942. A small number saw wartime service. Large-scale production began in 1945 when over 250 were built for the RAF and BOAC, and later many former RAF machines saw service with British and overseas operators. Pictured here is a York at Blackbushe Airport, Hampshire, in January 1952. The Fido fog dispersal system is being used: this was invented during the war and involved fuel feed through pipeline to burner jets placed adjacent to the runway.

The Yakovlev Yak-11 was first produced in 1946; this Russian two-seat military trainer with retractable undercarriage was powered by one 730hp Shvetsov Ash-21 engine. Today modified versions of the Yak-11 are popular with air race enthusiasts, and others have been repainted as "war birds". Shown here is a Czech-built C-11 version, photographed at the Biggin Hill air show on 11 May 1975.

The Short S25 Sandringham was a derivative of the Second World War long-range Sunderland flying boat that provided seating for 24 passengers on BOAC's routes to the Far East and Australia. It was also used by airlines in Australia and New Zealand. When this one was photographed on 6 April 1982 it was the last one still flying; it was originally operated by the New Zealand Air Force. Seen here taxiing under Tower Bridge in London, the aircraft is now in Kermit Weeks' Fantasy of Flight Museum in Florida.

This Canadair C-4 transport was developed in Canada; based on the American Douglas DC-4, the C-4 was powered by four Rolls-Royce Merlin engines. Its first flight was on 20 July 1946 and it was initially operated by BOAC, Trans Canada Air (TCA) Lines and the Canadian Air Force, who between them had the total production of 71. Known as the Argonaut with BOAC, it continued in service until 1958 when BOAC sold it to other operators. This photograph was taken at Heathrow where the aircraft was demonstrating the lifting by air cushion of damaged aircraft.

The Douglas C-47 Dakota became the most used and well-known twin engine transport after its first flight on 17 December 1935. Throughout the Second World War it performed countless missions and afterwards with over 1,000 different airlines across the world – where some are still in service today. This Railway Air Services Dakota met its untimely end on 19 December 1946 when it crashed on houses near Northolt Aerodrome en route for Glasgow. It had tried to take off when almost completely covered in snow; amazingly there was no loss of life.

The Airspeed AS57 Ambassador was a high-wing cantilever monoplane with two Bristol Centaurus engines with seating for up to 55 passengers. First flown by George Errington at Christchurch, Hampshire, on 10 July 1947, it suffered a number of problems during development, which resulted in only 21 being built and eventually entering service in 1951 with BEA. Disposed of in 1957, they continued in service with other operators, in particular Dan-Air, until the late 1960s. This version was fitted with Napier Eland engines, for experimental purposes, photographed here making a fly-by at Farnborough in September 1956.

The Bristol Type 171, a four-seat helicopter powered by an Alvis Leonides engine, was the first helicopter produced by Raoul Hafner and the helicopter division of the Bristol Helicopter Company; the original Mk1 version making a first flight on 27 July 1947. It was the first British-built helicopter to receive a Certificate of Airworthiness. When production ended in 1959 some 180 had been built for both civil and military operation. This Mk4 version was photographed in September 1954 at Farnborough.

N37602

The Hughes A-4 *Spruce Goose* NX37602, a wooden flying boat with eight engines, flew only once, on 2 November 1947. Piloted by Howard Hughes it lifted clear of the water to about 70ft for just over one mile. Designed to carry 750 passengers or 35 tons of cargo over a limited range, it holds the record for the largest wing-span at 320ft. It is shown here under tow at Long Beach, California, on 3 October 1980, to be exhibited alongside the liner *Queen Mary*. It is now in the Evergreen Aviation & Space Museum at McMinnville, Oregon.

The Vickers Viscount was a great British success story. This Viscount 700, named *Endeavour*, was photographed prior to departure in the London-New Zealand air race on 12 October 1953. Jointly entered by Vickers and BEA, and flown by Captain W Baillie and crew, it took 40 hours 41 minutes to cover the 12,365 miles to Christchurch. The flight helped to promote this turbo-prop aircraft powered by four Rolls-Royce Dart engines to become the most successful aircraft to emerge from post-war Britain.

Over 450 Viscounts were built by the time construction ceased in 1959 – more than any other British airliner. The first flight of the original series 630 aircraft, a 32-seat version, was from Wisley, Surrey on 16 July 1948; by the time the 800 series appeared the seating had increased to 86. Operated throughout the world by numerous airlines, a few can still be seen flying today.

This mammoth aircraft, with a wingspan of 230ft and fuselage length 177ft, was the largest landplane ever built in Britain; it's a Bristol Type 167 Brabazon and has eight Bristol Centaurus engines driving four pairs of contra-rotating propellers. Constructed at Filton in Bristol between 1944 and 1949 it cost £3 million (almost £300 million today) and was projected to carry an economical load from London to New York. This photo is from 4 September 1949 during its first flight, with A J (Bill) Pegg at the controls. It failed to live up to expectations and all work was suspended in 1952. The aircraft, and a partly built second one, was broken up a year later.

The Short S45 Solent 2 was the last of the large flying boats
flown by BOAC on overseas routes; it first flew in 1946 and
the last one was built in 1949. A total of 21 various marks
were produced, each carrying 34 passengers and 7 crew.
This photograph was taken on 5 May 1949 on the Thames
near the Tower of London for the aircraft to be named
City of London by the Lord Mayor, Sir George Aylwen, in
celebration of 30 years of British civil air transport.

De Havilland DH106 Comet 1 G-ALVG, the prototype of the first jet airliner in the world. This British-built aircraft, fitted with four DH Ghost 50 engines, was taken on its first flight from Hatfield, Hertfordshire on 27 July 1949 by John Cunningham. Development exceeded all expectations and the first of nine Comets were delivered to BOAC in early 1951. The first scheduled service to Johannesburg took place in May 1952; the first time a jet airliner had carried fare-paying passengers. Disaster followed, as a result of a number of unexplained accidents: structural failure caused by metal fatigue was discovered to be the reason. This photo was taken at the Farnborough air show in September 1949, just two months after first flight.

Westland Helicopters at Yeovil in Somerset built the Westland-Sikorsky WS51 under licence from the American company Sikorsky; it was one of the more successful early helicopters. When production ceased in 1953 around 139 had been built. This photo shows the WS51 leaving the village green at Nether Compton, Devon, in the early 1950s.

G-ALIK

The Lockheed L-1049 Super Constellation first flew in 1951, one of the most attractive variants that developed from the L-049, which dates from 1943. The L-1049 could carry up to 109 passengers and could cruise at 376mph with a range of up to 5,840 miles; in all 856 variants were produced. This is a L-1049G variant of Air France, landing at London Heathrow in May 1961.

The *Bournemouth*, a non-rigid airship G, was 108ft long with a capacity of 45,000 cu ft. When it took off at Cardington, Bedford, on 19 July 1951 it became the first to have flown in Britain since the R101. It had a crew of three, which unfortunately did not include its designer, Lord Ventry, since he was overweight at 17 stone. The aircraft was supported by the town of Bournemouth and others as a part of the Festival of Britain.

BOURNEMOUTH

G-AMJH

This De Havilland DH114 Heron four-engine feeder-liner was a development of the twin-engine Dove. It carried up to 17 passengers and the Mk1 version had a fixed undercarriage; it made its first flight from Hatfield on 10 May 1950. The Mk2, with retractable undercarriage, flew for the first time on 14 December 1952. Used by many British airlines and throughout the world, when production ceased around 150 had been produced; some are still flying. Pictured here at the SBAC show at Farnborough in September 1954 is one of seven Mk2Bs supplied to Turkish Airlines. The last scheduled flight from Croydon Airport, the scene of so much pre-war aviation, was a Heron 1b on 30 September 1959.

1952

This Saro S45 Princess flying boat with its 10 Bristol Proteus 600 propeller-jet engines was designed in an attempt to recreate the pre-war success of the flying boats that serviced Britain's empire. Designed to carry 200 passengers it was ordered by the government for BOAC. First flown by Geoffrey Tyson on 22 August 1952, it appeared a month later at Farnborough and again the next year, but by 1954 was cocooned at Cowes, on the Isle of Wight; interest in flying boats had waned. Two further examples were produced, but neither flew and they too were cocooned before all three were scrapped in 1967 after all attempts to find a buyer had failed. It is photographed here being launched at Cowes on 20 August 1952.

The De Havilland DHC3 Otter was built by DH Canada in 1952 for use in remote and extreme environments; 460 of these short take-off and landing aircraft were built. With a 600hp Pratt & Whitney R-1340 piston engine, it had seating for 11 passengers, and could operate on wheels, floats and snow undercarriages. Shown here is the Otter, unloading supplies on 10 January 1956, for the Trans-Antarctic Expedition, which was attempting the first surface crossing of the Antarctic.

This Bristol Type 173 helicopter was designed by Raoul Hafner, and was the first tandem-rotor, twin-engine helicopter built and flown in Britain. Ambitious in concept, with a long thin fuselage, it could carry 13 passengers and a crew of two and was powered by Alvis Leonides Major engines. Together with a number of others, this experimental helicopter failed to attract sufficient interest from buyers and so did not enter commercial production. It is shown here at the SBAC show at Farnborough on 2 September 1952, following its first flight at Filton, Bristol by C T D (Sox) Hosegood on 24 August.

This Bristol Type 175 Britannia 100 was developed as a medium-range transport for BOAC. First flown at Filton, Bristol by A J (Bill) Pegg on 16 August 1952, this 83-seat aircraft suffered many problems during development so that introduction into service with BOAC was delayed. The stretched 300 series found favour with a number of overseas operators as well as the Royal Air Force; eventually a total of 82 Britannias were built. Photographed here at Farnborough in September 1955 is the first prototype, painted in the colours of BOAC.

The Tupolev Tu-104, the first Russian-built jet liner, was based on the Tu-16 bomber. It could carry 50 passengers and five crew. The arrival of the prototype CCCP-L5400 at Heathrow on 22 March 1956 was a complete surprise, since its existence had, until then, been unknown. Pictured here at Heathrow a month later, on 25 April 1956, are the prototype along with two others that had brought food and passengers, including the Russian Secret Police Chief Serov who was accompanying Khrushchev, the Soviet leader, on a visit to London.

The Boeing 707 was first flown on 20 December 1957; originally built for 180 passengers, this was later increased as further variants were produced. A total of 1,010 have been operated worldwide for both civil and military purposes, although engine noise restrictions have prevented most from flying. A TWA Boeing 707 is shown here at Heathrow with the extra personnel needed to operate the Boeing 747 Jumbo Jet when it entered service in 1970.

The first Comet 4 flew on 27 April 1958, with deliveries to BOAC beginning in September. On 4 October of that year two Comet 4s made the first commercial jet service across the North Atlantic, one eastbound the other west – and in doing so they beat the Boeing 707 of the American airline PanAm by three weeks. 1958 was the first year that more people crossed the Atlantic by plane than by boat.

A four-cylinder VW car engine powered this Druine D31 Turbulent, designed by Frenchman Roger Druine, principally as a home-built aircraft. It had a wingspan of 20ft and cruised at 75mph; many have been constructed since they first flew in the late 1950s and are still flying today. The aircraft is pictured here beneath the nose of a Dakota at Croydon Airport on New Year's Day 1958, after the maiden flight of the first to be built in Britain by Rollason Aircraft & Engines. Norman Jōnes, chairman of Rollason, is seen here in the cockpit shortly after landing.

The Wessex helicopter was developed from the Sikorsky S-58 by Westland Helicopters at Yeovil as a two-crew, 12-passenger helicopter for both civil and military purposes. First flown in June 1958, fitted with a Napier Gazelle turbine, they found a particular niche for oilrig support. Pictured in Belgravia, London, early one Sunday morning in September 1973, a Wessex operated by Bristow Helicopters delivers three giant generators on to the roof of the Carlton Towers Hotel in 12 minutes; it would have taken three days, and considerable traffic chaos, if a crane had been used instead.

The Piper PA-25 Pawnee began life as an agricultural aircraft for crop spraying and associated tasks, but in Britain it found a new use as a glider-tug. First flown in 1959, this single-seat aircraft can be found all over the world. Photographed at Brunton airfield in May 2003, this Pawnee is doing what most of the 40 currently based in the UK do best.

1960

The McDonnell Douglas DC-8 was the principal competitor to the Boeing 707. First flown on 30 May 1958, it was powered by four 18,000lb Pratt & Whitney JT3D turbo fan engines, giving it a range of around 5,000 miles. Later versions had a longer fuselage with an increased passenger load; when production ceased in May 1972, some 556 had been delivered to 48 operators in 28 countries. Here one of the early variants of TCA prepares to leave London Heathrow in June 1960.

The Vickers Vanguard with its four Rolls-Royce Tyne engines was built to the order of BEA as a successor to the smaller Viscount. Flown for the first time from Brooklands, Surrey, on 20 January 1959, it did not find great favour – its total production run was only 44 aircraft, the only further order coming from TCA. Continuing to fly into the late 1990s, it found a role as a freighter. It is shown here in the colours of TCA at Farnborough in September 1960.

This Wallis WA-116 Agile single-seat autogyro with a 72hp engine was one of a series of such machines designed by Wing Commander Ken Wallis in Norfolk. Pictured here is G-ARZB, built at Shoreham by Beagle Aircraft, being flown by its designer in August 1967, having recently appeared in the James Bond film *You Only Live Twice* as *Little Nellie*.

This is a Hawker Siddeley (DH 121) Trident built to a BEA specification for a short-haul jet transport, making its first flight from Hatfield on 9 January 1962. Fitted with three Rolls-Royce Spey engines, it could seat up to 103. Later variants were to follow, with orders from a number of overseas operators including 35 for China; ultimately 117 were built. Piloted by John Cunningham, De Havilland's chief test pilot, the first flight was watched by Sir Geoffrey De Havilland. It is almost 51 years to the day since the president of the company flew the DH 1, which had a top speed of 40mph; the Trident cruised at about 600mph.

1962

The majestic-looking Vickers VC10 was powered by four Rolls-Royce Conway turbo fans. Built for BOAC's long-distance routes, its seating for up to 174 passengers, short field performance and superb handling near the ground were some of its major selling points. Services to Lagos began in April 1964 and to New York (with a Super version) on 1 April 1965. Although only 65 of the Standard and Super variants were produced there is no doubting the quality of the aircraft – only the operating costs prevented more being sold. Many went into service with the RAF in the transport and refuelling role; some are still active today. This is the prototype on its first take-off from Brooklands on 29 June 1962 in the hands of Jock Bryce.

The BAC 1-11 was initially built as a 79-seat short-haul airliner with Rolls-Royce Spey engines; the first order for 10 aircraft came from British United Airways (BUA). Pictured here is the prototype series 200 aircraft landing after its first flight at Hurn Airport, Bournemouth, on 20 August 1963 in the hands of Jock Bryce, chief test pilot and his deputy, Mike Lithgow. Further orders followed from airlines worldwide, including some in the United States; new and larger variants appeared, eventually leading to a total production of 244, including a small number built in Romania.

1963

The Boeing 727 first flew on 9 February 1963; when production ceased on 18 September 1984, some 1,832 of all variants had been produced for airlines throughout the world. This American-built three-engine airliner with Pratt & Whitney JT8D engines had seating for a maximum of 189 passengers, and three crew. Pictured here in August 1989 is a 727 of the German airline Lufthansa.

The Santos-Dumont Demoiselle was a forerunner of the ultra-light aircraft that have now become so popular. It was built by Doug Bianchi at Personal Plane Services as a replica of a 1910 aircraft for the film *Those Magnificent Men and Their Flying Machines*. Fitted with a 50hp Ardem engine, it was initially reluctant to leave the ground until it was remembered that Santos-Dumont was a small man. Joan Hughes, a former Second World War ATA pilot was recruited to fly it: here she is testing the Demoiselle; later she flew many of the other replicas used in the film.

The Britten-Norman BN-2 Islander, an all-metal, 10-seat short-haul aircraft took just 18 months to design, build and be successfully test flown. Its first flight was on 13 June 1965 from Bembridge, on the Isle of Wight; at the controls were its designers John Britten and Desmond Norman. Fitted originally with two Lycoming engines, later versions, which are still being constructed today, have Allison 250-B17 turboprops. Sold to almost every country in the world, the Islander has proved to have great performance characteristics: it is relatively cheap, has low operating costs and is easy to maintain. Over 1,250 have been produced so far, making it the best-selling commercial aircraft in Western Europe. Pictured at Farnborough in September 1966 are G-ATWU, the first production aircraft and G-ATCT, the unique short-span prototype.

The Aero Spaceline Super Guppy was designed on the airframe of the Boeing Stratocruiser for carrying outsized cargo components. It could carry 18,000kgs of freight while cruising at 300mph with a maximum range of almost 2,000 miles. In the early 1970s Airbus Industries acquired four aircraft to carry components of the decentralised Airbus production lines. This former Airbus Industries Super Guppy is now preserved by the British Aviation Heritage at Bruntingthorpe, Leicestershire.

The McDonnell Douglas DC9 twin-engine airliner first flew in 1965; it subsequently became the basis for the MD-80, MD-90 and Boeing 717, the last one of which was delivered in 2006. The first DC-9 entered service with Delta Airline in America in late 1965, by the time production of the DC-9 finished in 1982 almost 1,000 had been built, with about a quarter still in service with the world's airlines. Photographed here is an Alitalia DC-9 landing at Heathrow Airport in 1992.

This Lebaudy Replica Airship was a 137ft long dirigible and featured in the film *Chitty, Chitty Bang Bang*. It was constructed at Cardington, Bedford, in the sheds in which the R101 was built. It's pictured here on a farm at Turville Heath, Buckinghamshire, from where the first flight was made on 9 August 1967. Lionel Jeffries, one of the film's stars, is seen here giving it a tow! This delightful and much loved film also starred Dick Van Dyke and Sally Ann Howes.

The Boeing 737 is the *baby* of the Boeing family of commercial jet-transport aircraft. It first flew, as the series 100, on 9 April 1967 following an order from Lufthansa. Development has now reached the series 800, with passenger seating ranging from 115 to 150. Production continues, with over 5,000 of these versatile aircraft having been built. Pictured here at Newcastle is one of easyJet's 30-strong fleet of 737s.

Here is the Handley Page HP137 Jetstream in which John Allum made the first flight on 18 August 1967 following its roll out at Radlett, Hertfordshire on 29 June. Following the demise of Handley Page, production resumed with Scottish Aviation, who later became part of British Aerospace (BAe). The aircraft was progressively developed into the Jetstream 31 and 41 series, finding buyers worldwide as a feeder-liner or executive transport; a total of 465 were built, and many are still in service today.

1967

The Tupalov Tu-144 supersonic transport was similar in design to the Concorde, and designed to carry 140 passengers. Its initial flight on 31 December 1968 made it the world's first supersonic transport to fly; it first flew at the speed of sound on 5 June 1969. It was put into service by Aeroflot for scheduled freight operation in December 1975 between Moscow and Alma Ata, and passenger flights followed in November 1977. A total of 17 were built, but after three unfortunate accidents the Concordski was eventually withdrawn from service. One is shown here at the Paris air show in June 1971.

The iconic BAe/Aerospatiale Concorde was the first and only successful supersonic commercial airliner – so far. The Anglo-French project saw the 001, the French-built aircraft, fly first on 2 March 1969, piloted by Andre Turcat for a 42 minute flight. After testing and protracted negotiations British Airways and Air France began services between London and New York in 1976. A total of 20 were completed, operating from London and Paris to New York until all operations ceased on 24 October 2004, with a last flight on 26 November; services to other cities stopped much earlier. Pictured here is the British-built Concorde 002 G-BSST taking off from Filton, Bristol, on 9 April 1969: it is flown by Brian Trubshaw for the first flight of 20 minutes. This aircraft is preserved in the Fleet Air Arm Museum at Yeovilton.

The Boeing 747 revolutionised long-haul air travel with its ability to carry up to around 500 passengers in its vast fuselage and upper deck. Powered by a variety of engines, it became known as the 'Jumbo Jet' after a first flight on 9 February 1969. Developed further into the 300 and 400 series, it has been operated by most major airlines in the world. Shown here is the arrival of the first 747 in Britain on a proving flight at London Heathrow from New York on 12 January 1970; PanAm operated their first passenger service on 21 January 1970.

The McDonnell-Douglas DC-10 was first flown on 29 August 1970; with three General Electric CF6 engines it had a range of 4,606 miles, carrying up to 345 passengers. It first entered service with American Airlines on 5 August 1971; eventually 446 were sold to numerous airlines worldwide. This Laker Airways DC-10 is in its famous Skytrain livery at Gatwick, photographed on 16 January 1975.

The Bede BD5J mini-jet, powered by a Microturbo TRS-18-046 engine, was designed by Jim Bede as a homebuilt kit to be the smallest jet in the world. It was 12ft 4in long and 5ft 1in high. Pictured here at Farnborough in September 1976, a French-built version is dwarfed by an Airbus A300.

The Goodyear Tyre & Rubber Co involvement with airships used for advertising goes back to 1925. From 1968 new versions appeared, about 200ft long with a diameter of 50ft, powered by two 210hp Continental engines giving an endurance of 20 hours. The airship could carry six passengers and was frequently used as a television platform covering major sporting and other events. Pictured at Cardington being hauled into position on 9 March 1972 is the N-2A *Europa*, which regularly toured Britain and Europe.

EUROPA
N2A

GOOD YEAR

De Havilland DHC-7 *Dash-7* was a short-range STOL commuter airliner built in Canada with two Pratt & Whitney PT6 turboprops. First flown on 27 March 1975, this aircraft proved popular with many airlines but is now superseded by the Dash-8. Pictured on 31 May 1987 is a Eurocity Express aircraft making the first trial landings at the London City Airport built on the former docks in East London. Many considered the airport something of a white elephant in its early days, but it now handles over 3 million passengers a year.

This Boeing B-747 N905NA shuttle carrier with Space Shuttle *Enterprise* above
is used by NASA to transport orbiters over long distances. The 747 is a modified
ex-American Airlines aircraft. The pair first flew together in 1978. When carrying a
Shuttle the B-747 is limited to a range of 1,150 miles and a ceiling of 15,000ft. They
are pictured at RAF Station, Fairford, Gloucestershire, during the International Air
Tattoo in May 1983 where it made a short stop en route to Bonn and Paris.

The Antonov An-74 Stol transport, powered by two Lotarev D-36 turbofans, was built in Russia for civil and military use. It can seat 36 to 86 passengers but has found good use as a freighter. Its first flight was on 31 August 1977; this photo was taken at the Farnborough air show in September 1998.

British Aerospace BAe 146 feeder-jet transport had a long and complicated history, beginning in the 1960s, leading to the first flight of the series 100 from Hatfield in September 1981. It was sold around the world and ultimately almost 400 were built. This is the series 300 G-5-300 on take-off from Hatfield for a first flight on 1 May 1987.

The Airbus A320 is the third of the Airbus family of airlines that first flew at Toulouse, France, on 22 February 1987. It operates with two-crew, and this short-medium range airliner can carry 150 passengers with two CFM56 engines over a 2,900 mile range. Air France was the first customer for the aircraft, which have sold over 1,000 to date; it is shown here on take-off at London Heathrow in November 1992.

Skyship Airship *Spirit of Dubai* promoting the Palm Island project, pictured over London, close to Canary Wharf and the Dome, in November 2006 before departing to Europe en route to Dubai. It is the largest commercial airship in the world at 66m long and 22m high, and cruises at 40mph. It proves the enduring appeal of the airship, particularly as an advertising platform.

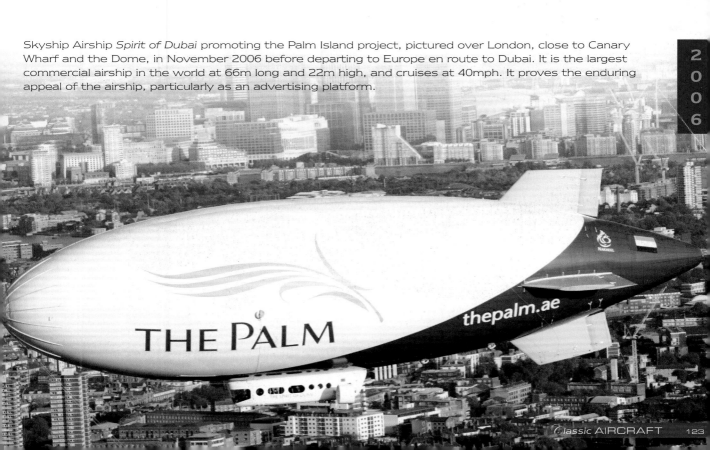

Concorde taking off at London's Heathrow on a test flight in July 2001 following the crash of an Air France aircraft in Paris the previous year.

The Concorde made a Farewell Tour in October 2003; it's seen here landing at Belfast's Aldergrove Airport.

The last scheduled Concorde flight from New York lands at Heathrow on 24 October 2003.

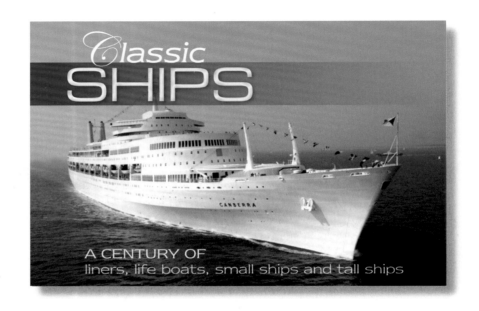

Classic
SHIPS

A CENTURY OF
liners, life boats, small ships and tall ships

Available from all major stockists